BRITISH FLOAT PLANES

K
3641

BRITISH FLOAT PLANES

A PICTORIAL SURVEY

G. R. DUVAL AFM

D. BRADFORD BARTON LIMITED

© *copyright D. Bradford Barton 1976*   *ISBN 0 85153 255 1*

printed in Great Britain by H. E. Warne Ltd, London and St. Austell

for the publishers

D .BRADFORD BARTON LTD · Trethellan House · Truro · Cornwall · England

foreword

As a seafaring nation, it is hardly surprising that Britain at one time led the world in design and construction of marine aircraft, both flying-boats and floatplanes, and since the former has already formed the subject for a book in this series, this volume has been prepared to complete the story. Essentially, the floatplane was a modification of the landplane for marine use, and as such the prospects of development were limited. In direct contrast to the flying-boat, the floatplane found little civil use in this country, but gave magnificent service in World War I and the inter-war period. Its most significant contribution to aviation development resulted directly from the Schneider Trophy contests, which accelerated airframe and engine efficiency far beyond normal progress for the period, paving the way for the fighter aircraft that so ably defended this country in 1940.

I am again indebted to Mr Bruce Robertson for his assistance in compiling this book, and the publishers, and I would like to thank the following organisations for help so generously given: The Blackburn and de Havilland Divisions of the British Aircraft Corporation, Hawker Siddeley Aviation, the Ministry of Defence, and the Canadian National Archives.

G. R. Duval

Watton, Norfolk

The Fairey IIID of 1921, powered by a Napier Lion engine.

overleaf ▷

The Short S.7 Mussel I, registered G-EBMJ, was a two-seater floatplane with metal fuselage and floats, the engine being a 60 h.p. A.D.C. Cirrus I. Built at Rochester in 1925, the Mussel did not enter production, but in 1928 it broke the world record for its class, with a flight to 13,400 feet.

introduction

By the year of 1909, with aviation in its infancy and crashes the rule rather than the exception, a growing body of opinion amongst aircraft designers gave voice to the opinion that flying from water would be safer. This, plus the characteristic of the human race to make progress through experimentation, led to the first crude adaptation of an early aircraft for marine flying by substituting pontoons or floats for the normal land undercarriage. The very first of these machines was an incredible construction on the canard, or tail-first, principle, by M. Henri Fabre in France, and the maiden flight took place on 28 March 1910. In July of the following year, Glenn Curtiss flew his A-1 floatplane in America, and in November of that year an Avro machine made the first British off-water flight at Barrow-in-Furness, followed a week later by a second Avro machine at Lake Windermere.

At this juncture, it is perhaps apposite to clarify the terms used in Britain to identify marine aircraft. Up to 1913, all marine aircraft were referred to collectively as 'hydro-aeroplanes' or sometimes 'hydro-planes'. As the Secretary of State for the Admiralty, the late Sir Winston Churchill suggested the term 'seaplane' and this was officially adopted. This general reference was sub-divided by general consent into 'floatplane' for aeroplanes equipped with float undercarriages, and 'flying-boat' for types in which the fuselage constituted a hull. For some reason, the Admiralty never recognised the term 'flying-boat' and referred to this class as 'boat-seaplanes'.

In the days leading up to the first World War, the Avro, Short and Sopwith companies all built experimental floatplanes, the majority of which were conversions of land machines. A number of these floatplanes were purchased by the Admiralty for the embryo Royal Naval Air Service, formed on 13 May 1912 as the Naval Wing, Royal Flying Corps. This formation was in the face of the scepticism voiced by some senior officers, as had happened with the Royal Flying Corps, but fortunately for this country, the Air Department of the Admiralty had a far-seeing Director in Captain Murray Sueter, enthusiastically supported by the First Lord, Winston Churchill. Additionally, the capabilities of the floatplane were adequately demonstrated by Harry Hawker's magnificent flight in a Sopwith machine as the sole contender for the *Daily Mail* 'Circuit of Britain' prize in 1913, when 1,043 miles of coastal flying was completed in just three days. The adoption of the floatplane by the Royal Navy was not just the addition of another weapon to the World's greatest sea power of the time, but in furtherance of an idea first mooted in 1911 by Lt. Hyde-Thomson, RN, concerning the possibility of dropping a torpedo from an aircraft. It should be remembered that at this time, the torpedo was a comparatively new naval weapon, and its delivery from the air would mean a vast extension of its capability in that just one aeroplane could sink a war or merchant ship of several thousand tons. Both the Sopwith and Short companies were contracted by the Admiralty to built torpedo-carrying floatplanes, and in the event the Short machine was adopted for production, eventually to become the R.N.A.S. 'workhorse' as the famous Short 184. This torpedo-carrying requirement was the reason why the majority of British naval floatplanes of World War I were of large size and fitted with very powerful engines for the period.

From the outbreak of war on 4 August 1914, to 16 February 1916, the Admiralty were responsible for the air defence of the British Isles, and accordingly the R.N.A.S. strength steadily increased by orders for production flying-boats and floatplanes, as well as land-based aircraft. The floatplanes concerned began as a heterogeneous collection of early types, but by 1915 a powerful force of Wights, Sopwiths and the new Short 184s had gradually come into being for use on coastal patrol, a vital necessity, due to the activities of German U-Boats, which in those days were building up an ever-increasing concentration around the coasts of Britain, and attacking ships in the North and Irish Seas, the Channel and the Western Approaches. The R.N.A.S. floatplanes by no means confined themselves to patrol activity, and their use as bombers began in 1914 with a Christmas Day raid by Short machines and others on Cuxhaven. The somewhat limited range of the floatplanes was vastly increased by the use of carrier ships, which included special vessels, light cruisers and requisitioned paddle-steamers, the floatplanes being lowered to the water by crane and recovered after flight by the same means. This practice led indirectly to the first aircraft carrier take-offs in 1915 by the little Sopwith Schneider scouts, developed from the 1914 Schneider Trophy winner. In many attempts to intercept Zeppelins over the North Sea, the Schneiders had trouble with sea conditions and float damage, so a scheme was devised whereby the aircraft ook-off from special decks on wheeled trolleys.

On 12 August 1915, the hopes of the torpedo enthusiasts seemed to come to fruition, for on that date Flt. Cdr. Edmonds successfully launched a missile from his Short 184 and hit a Turkish supply ship; five days later he struck another, and Flt. Lt. Dacre torpedoed a steam tug. Unfortunately, these were the only attacks of this type by a British floatplane in World War I, for the huge weight of the weapons was just too much for the aircraft, which required a calm sea, a slight breeze, and drastic weight reduction of crew and petrol, even to become airborne. Another problem, which affected all types of floatplane in service in the Mediterranean, the Red Sea, and other tropical and semi-tropical areas was the effect of high temperatures on engine performance, for a long take-off run put great stress on the square-sectioned wooden floats of the day, often with disastrous results. Be that as it may, the floatplanes of the R.N.A.S. gave sterling service during World War I, covering thousands of miles on unspectacular patrols, bombing land and sea targets and attacking German U-Boats. On the last day of May 1916, a Short floatplane made the only reconnaissance flight of the sea action later recorded in history as the Battle of Jutland. A little more spice was added by the air-to-air fighting, mainly in the Eastern Mediterranean, by the pilots of the Sopwith Schneider scouts and their later development, the Sopwith Baby. Many of the latter type were built under sub-contract by two companies later responsible for much floatplane development, and whose names became synonymous with naval flying, those of Blackburn and Fairey. Both companies had built floatplane types for the R.N.A.S. in the later days of World War I, and amongst these the most significant was the Fairey N9, forerunner of the famous Fairey III series and participant in early catapult-launch trials, designed to obviate the tedious procedure of hoisting machines overboard from seaplane carriers, or flying-off from decks on wheeled trolleys.

With the Armistice of 1918, British naval aviation, now a part of the R.A.F., shrank to minute proportions, with floatplanes represented by just one Flight. On the civil side, several leading aircraft manufacturers made gallant attempts to introduce the floatplane to the civilian market, but with only very limited success. After failure with a racing floatplane for the 1919 Schneider Trophy, the Sopwith company vanished, to be replaced by Hawkers, who were concerned with land aircraft; Short Brothers took up flying-boat development; Avro left the marine field after producing some Avro 504 conversions and developments, and apart from the odd experimental types, most subsequent orders for floatplanes went to Blackburn and Fairey, who, from 1919 onwards set the fashion for many future designs in producing alternative wheel or float undercarriages. Thus, for sound business reasons, the pure floatplane ceased to exist, save for special reasons such as the racing machines produced for the Schneider Trophy contests. One of the last of the World War I floatplanes to see active service was the Fairey IIIC, several of which equipped part of the North Russian Expeditionary Force, based at Archangel in 1919. The Fairey IIID of 1920 featured in an important innovation of the postwar years, when, in 1925, a float-equippped machine of this type became the first standard F.A.A. aircraft to be catapult-launched from a warship, and thereafter this method of launching reconnaissance floatplanes from cruisers and battleships was extensively used.

In the mid-1920s, an experimental metal hull for the Short S.2 flying-boat proved entirely successful, and thereafter Short Brothers concentrated on metal construction which included the design and manufacture of floats for floatplanes. These floats were of far greater strength and hydrodynamic efficiency than their wooden predecessors, which now became obsolete. The new floats were tested on a Fairey Flycatcher, and the first production machine so equipped was one of the best-remembered naval, and R.A.F., aircraft of the inter-war period, the Fairey IIIF. One of the most dramatic illustrations of the strength of metal floats was the occasional practice of landing a floatplane on an aircraft carrier deck. After delivering its message or passenger, the machine would then be lowered to the water by crane, with the engine still running, and take-off for the return flight!

As has been stated, pure floatplane designs had by now become a rarity, appearing now and then in the experimental field or for a specific purpose. Examples of this are the Short Valetta, built to compare the large floatplane with the flying-boat, the Short Scion Senior, designed as a half-scale model of the Empire Flying-boat for aerodynamic tests, and the Parnall Peto, intended for operations from the ill-fated submarine, M.2, an idea stemming from German designs of World War I and finally put into practice by the Japanese in World War II. However, and without a doubt, the greatest contribution of the floatplane to aeronautical development concerned the Schneider Trophy contests, first flown in 1914, then from 1919 to 1931. The success of the American Curtiss racing floatplanes in 1923 caused British designers, notably R. J. Mitchell of the Supermarine company, to abandon the small flying-boat in favour of high-powered floatplanes, and since national prestige was at stake, no effort was spared. The first of the new British machines, the Supermarine S.4, flew at 226 m.p.h. in 1925, at which time R.A.F. fighters were achieving around 150 m.p.h. Two years later, the Gloster VI created a World record of 336 m.p.h., and in 1931 the Supermarine S.6B became the first aircraft in the world to exceed 400 m.p.h., its Rolls-Royce engine delivering a fantastic 2,600 h.p., albeit for a short period. In the same year, the Hawker Fury fighter made its maiden flight, achieving just 207 m.p.h. with a 525 h.p. engine. Throughout the Schneider Trophy period, British designers and their foreign competitors amassed a vast storehouse of constructional, aerodynamic and engine design knowledge, while the R.A.F. High Speed Flight gained invaluable experience in flying at airspeeds far in excess of normal for the period, comparable with the beginning of the jet age in later years. It is interesting to realise now, for example, that the problems of high-gravity loading which causes pilots to "black-out", that is, to lose vision, were first encountered and overcome some forty years ago in racing floatplanes. One very tangible result of British Schneider Trophy experience was R. J. Mitchell's immortal Spitfire, together with its Rolls-Royce Merlin engine. As a footnote, it may be recorded that the Contests, especially in their later years, were of great attraction and interest to the general public, and the sight of these beautifully streamlined machines in their bright colour-schemes, at full speed, must have been an unforgettable experience.

In the late-1930s, with the value of aircraft-carriers becoming apparent in naval circles, the use of the floatplane began to decline, although the fast Hawker Osprey, together with Blackburn's Shark and the famous Swordfish, were still serving in some numbers, both in warships and shore-based. The last pure floatplane design by a British manufacturer for naval use was the Fairey Seafox, which echoed the sole Short 184 flight of the Battle of Jutland in spotting for the guns of *Ajax, Achilles* and *Exeter,* during the Battle of the River Plate in December 1939, which resulted in the destruction of the German battleship *Graf Spee*. On the civil side, a number of de Havilland landplanes were converted to floatplanes for use on the Canadian lakes and rivers, and the last British civil floatplane took to the air in 1937 as "Mercury", upper portion of the successful Short-Mayo Composite aircraft and holder to this day of the World long-distance record in its category. During World War II, the decline of the floatplane accelerated rapidly, and few remained in service after 1940, their duties being taken over by flying-boats and carrier-borne landplanes more suitable for open-sea operation. An interesting experiment of the war years was the conversion of two Marks of Spitfire to floatplanes, with a view to providing fighter cover in campaigns beyond the range of land-based aircraft, such as in Norway, but by the time the machines had been evaluated the requirement had lapsed. After the war, two float-equipped Auster A.O.P.6 aircraft made the last British service flights of this type of aircraft in support of the R.A.F. Antartic Expedition of 1949-50. The de Havilland Tiger Moth had seen long service with the Navy and R.A.F. as a pilotless radio-controlled target floatplane, and in 1963 the newly-founded British Seaplane Club fitted one example of this superb little aircraft with floats again, as the last floatplane of all.

The Wight Pusher Floatplane at the Olympia Air Show of 1913. The German and British Navies each purchased one machine, with a further British order for ten following evaluation of the first, No. 155. The engine was a 200 h.p. Canton Unne.

The first floatplane experiments by Short Brothers were made in 1912, using the Tractor Biplane of 1910 fitted with a central float and stabilising airbags under the wings. The engine was a 70 h.p. Gnome rotary and the machine had two seats. It was purchased by the Admiralty as their No. 5.

Commander Samson, R.N. with Sir Winston Churchill (then First Lord of the Admiralty) aboard a Short 74 in July 1914. The Short 74 was an improved version of the earlier S.41 fitted with a 100 h.p. Gnome engine, the first aircraft, No. 74, being erected at Leven in March 1914. Three machines of this type, but with 160 h.p. engines, formed part of a formation which bombed the airship sheds at Cuxhaven on Christmas Day, 1914.

Before and during World War I, Lake Windermere saw a good deal of experimental and instructional flying with marine aircraft. The Blackburn Moreland Sea Trainer is shown here on the Lake in 1915. This machine was a development of the 1912 Monoplane, fitted originally with an 80 h.p. Gnôme but later re-engined with a 100 h.p. Anzani. It may be noted that the land undercarriage skids have been retained.

The Avro Type 503 Waterplane, seen after acceptance tests at Volk's Seaplane Base, Brighton, in June 1913. Two years before, its predecessor, the Avro Hydro-plane, had made the first successful British flight from water. Powered by a 100 h.p. engine the Type 503 was one of a number of Avro biplane designs which led to the famous Avro 504.

The Sopwith entrant for the 1913 Circuit of Britain Race, sponsored by the *Daily Mail.* The machine had a 100 h.p. Green engine and was flown by Harry Hawker, who covered 1,043 miles before crashing at Loughshinny in Ireland.

A Wight Pusher Floatplane being hoisted aboard a ship of the Royal Navy, probably the *Ark Royal*. The ten Wights ordered by the Navy all had extended wings which were rigged to fold, as seen here, plus other modifications for naval duties.

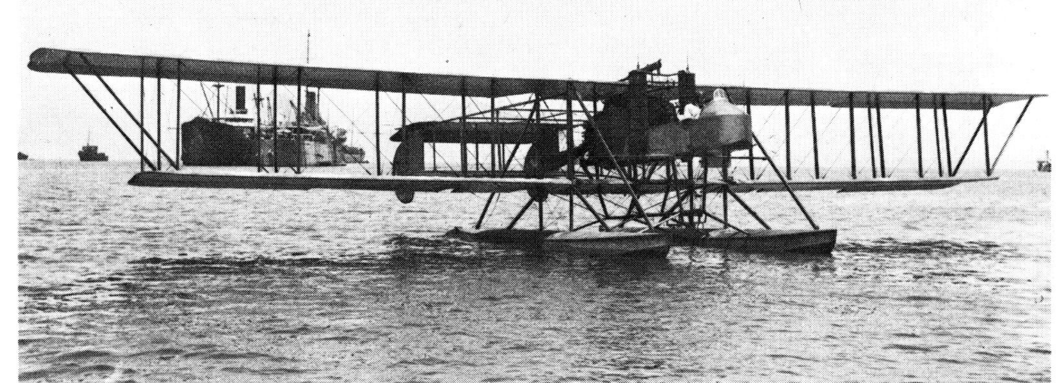

Wight Floatplane No. 176 on the water with wings extended, giving a good idea of its size and the multitude of struts. With a 200 h.p. engine, the Wight was a powerful machine for its day, and at least two operated in the Dardanelles campaign.

In 1913 the Royal Aircraft Factory built the H.R.E.2— Hydro Reconnaissance Experimental No. 2. This was an R.E.1 landplane fitted with floats for trial purposes, the results of which were not inspiring, the machine being re-converted.

The Sopwith *Daily Mail* Circuit of Britain machine at Scarborough on 25 August 1913. The flight made by Hawker on this day, from the Solent via the East Coast to Beadnell was a world's record for one day's over-sea flying.

Hawker's performance in the 'Circuit' floatplane made a great impression on the Amiralty, and, as the original had been wrecked, a second machine was ordered for the R.N.A.S. as their No. 151, which is shown here. It later served with No. 4 Wing.

The Sopwith entry for the 1914 Schneider Trophy contest at Monaco was this modified Tabloid, fitted with a 100 h.p. Gnome engine and flown by Howard Pixton. The race was won by Pixton, who then created a world record at 92 m.p.h.

At the outbreak of war in 1914, the R.N.A.S. quickly adopted the superb little Schneider Tabloid for scouting purposes, and production commenced in November 1914. The early production machines differed little from the original, but in later aircraft the tail-fin was enlarged and ailerons replaced the wing-warping control system.

A Sopwith Schneider under test on the Thames, complete with interested spectators. Altogether, 160 Schneiders were built, and although somewhat hampered by rough sea conditions in the North Sea, they did much useful work in the eastern Mediterranean and Red Sea areas, also in the Dardanelles. Their armament comprised one Lewis gun mounted on the centre section, and provision for a 65-pound bomb below the fuselage.

A 1915 scene at Messrs R. J. Turk & Sons' boatyard on the Thames, situated near the Sopwith Works at Kingston. The facilities of this yard, together with its slipways, were made available for the flotation tests of production floatplanes. Two late-production aircraft are seen here; in R.N.A.S. service they were known as Sopwith Schneiders.

The Sopwith 860 appeared in late-1914, powered by the 225 h.p. Sunbeam engine and designed to carry an 810-pound 14-inch torpedo. Eighteen of these aircraft were delivered to the R.N.A.S. who used them on patrols in home waters during 1915 and 1916, but the type, although aerodynamically sound, suffered a great deal from engine failures.

The Short Admiralty Type 827 was first ordered for the R.N.A.S. in the summer of 1914; ultimately over 100 were built. Powered by a 150 h.p. Sunbeam, the 827 had a long life, serving from 1915 until the Armistice both at home and overseas bases.

Seen here at Cowes in early 1914, the Sopwith Type C floatplane was built for the Admiralty and taken on their charge as No. 138 at Calshot. The 200 h.p. Salmson engine was fitted with an extension shaft to permit a more streamlined fairing, and the machine featured a patent torpedo-dropping mechanism between the floats.

Sponsored by the Air Department of the Admiralty, the A.D. Naviplane was built by Supermarines in eight weeks and flown to the Isle of Grain in mid-1917 for testing. Following two engine failures, the type was abandoned due to poor performance.

Developed from the 1915 Sopwith Schneider, the Sopwith Baby had a 110 h.p. Clerget engine, and most aircraft were armed with a synchronised Lewis gun. Production was taken over by the Blackburn Company, who built 186 machines.

A Blackburn-built Baby being serviced ashore. The last 115 machines from this company were powered by a 130 h.p. Clerget engine, and some carried Rankin anti-Zeppelin darts in place of a Lewis gun. Two 65-pound bombs were carried.

The machines built by the Fairey Company to the basic Sopwith design were known as Hamble Babies, and one such is shown here. While giving useful service in the Middle East and Mediterranean areas, the Babies were extremely active in the anti-submarine role around the coasts of Britain, and made many attacks on U-Boats.

A Blackburn Baby, armed unusually with two Lewis guns and one 65-pound bomb. This particular machine flew anti-U-Boat patrols from Hornsea Mere, a Yorkshire lake chosen for sheltered waters, and near the coastal patrol area.

Sopwith Type 860 No. 851 after launching from the slipway, and giving a good indication of its large size. This machine was under test following completion in late-1914 and it survived until March 1917, when it was finally written-off.

Above and opposite: The Blackburn TB twin-engined twin fuselage biplane. This unique design was produced to meet Admiralty requirements for an anti-Zeppelin machine, and was powered by two 100 h.p. Gnôme engines. Nine of these aircraft were built, their sole armament comprising four boxes of Rankin anti-Zeppelin darts, but their performance was so poor that they were scrapped in September 1917.

The Wight "Converted" Seaplane was so named because it was a conversion of a landplane bomber which did not enter production. Although only 37 Wights were built, they did sterling work on coastal patrol, one of them destroying U-Boat *UB-32* in the English Channel. Below: Two Sopwith Type 807 floatplanes at Mafia island for operations against the German cruiser *Konigsberg* in the Rufigi Delta. These machines had folding wings and a 100 h.p. Gnôme engine.

Built by the Aircraft Manufacturing
Company, this Henri Farman,
N1530, was fitted with a 140 h.p.
Hispano engine and a float
undercarriage for the R.N.A.S.
in 1916. This was an experiment,
possibly to evaluate the aircraft
as a trainer.

The Fairey N9 and N10 were the
prototypes of the very famous
Fairey III series, and were fitted
with the 265 h.p. Sunbeam Maori
engine. N9, shown here, was used
in early catapult trials, while N10
was flown with floats, skids, and
wheeled undercarriage.

The large aircraft is the A.D.1000
of late-1914, armed with bombs
and a 12-pounder gun. Two of
these machines were built, but
proved to be underpowered and
were scrapped in 1917. On the
right is the Wight Baby single-
seater scout. This was
abandoned in 1917.

The Short 310/320 was the last of many floatplanes from this company to enter service during World War I, and was also the largest, designed for long range and a 1,000-pound torpedo armament. The type designation was derived from the engine, which in the original version was a 310 h.p. Sunbeam Cossack, later replaced by a 320 h.p. unit. The aircraft depicted here, N1597, was originally produced as a Short 184 by Frederick Sage & Co. Ltd., of Peterborough.

The Fairey Campania was the first machine specifically designed for operation from a seaplane carrier and derived its name from initial allocation to H.M.S. *Campania* in 1917. The fifth production machine, N1004, is seen here at the Isle of Grain in the summer of 1917, fitted with a 275 h.p. Rolls-Royce Eagle I engine, an enlarged fin and broad-chord ailerons. 42 Campanias were in service by the Armistice, with either Sunbeam Maori or Rolls-Royce Eagle engines.

Best-known of all World War I floatplanes of the R.N.A.S. was the Short 184, more than 650 of which were built to serve in practically every theatre of war. A Short 184 was the very first aircraft to sink a ship by torpedo, on 12 August 1915.

Built by Frederick Sage & Co., the Sage 4C of 1917 was intended as a trainer, being a floatplane version of the Sage Type 3 landplane. Delays caused by trouble with the 200 h.p. Hispano engine led to very late delivery, and the machine crashed in 1919.

Three Wight Baby single-seater scouts were built in 1917, numbered 9097, 9098 and 9100. The second machine went to the Isle of Grain experimental station, where it was extensively tested after modification, but the type was not accepted.

A Short 184 taking-off. Apart from its other claims to fame as the R.N.A.S. "workhorse" of World War I, the 184 was the only aircraft employed by either side in the Battle of Jutland, when one machine made a spotting flight from *Engadine*.

The Short N2B was the last wartime design by this company, and did not enter service. It was powered by the 260 h.p. Sunbeam, and six prototypes were ordered as an improvement on the Short 184. In the event, its performance fell short of requirements.

The immediate predecessor of the famous Short 184 was the Short 830, a smaller version of the earlier Type 166, and powered by the Canton Unne engine of 135 h.p. 28 of this type were built by Shorts, and 68 others were Sunbeam-engined as the 827.

The Blackburn S.P. Kangaroo No. 1416, powered by 190 h.p. Rolls-Royce Falcon II engines, was a second prototype, the first, No. 1415, having 225 h.p. Sunbeams. 10 machines of this type were converted to landplanes for maritime patrol, serving with No. 246 Squadron, R.A.F.

The de Havilland 4 served with distinction in the R.N.A.S., and amongst many actions, a machine of this type shot down Zeppelin *L70*. In 1917, trials were made with both the Sopwith Camel and DH.4 mounted on float undercarriages, but without notable success.

In 1919, a further version of the
famous Avro 504 was produced,
extending its scope to the field of
marine training and sports flying.
This was the Avro 504L, powered
by the 130 h.p. Clerget rotary
engine. A number of 504Ls saw
post-war civil flying usage.

The Avro Company was no stranger to the floatplane, with the first flight of this type in Britain to their credit. After the
war, the company employed many ex-R.A.F. personnel to give "joy-ride" passenger flights in Avro 504s, and two 504L
machines used for this purpose are seen here. The aircraft are from a cancelled contract.

This racing floatplane was built by Sopwith as an entrant in the 1919 Schneider Trophy race. Powered by a 450 h.p. Cosmos Jupiter radial engine the machine reached a speed of 180 m.p.h., but was dogged by trouble with the floats which caused its withdrawal. In the event, the contest was void.

The Vickers Vixen III, registered G-EBIP, was a floatplane variant of the Vixen II general-purpose landplane, with a 450 h.p. Napier Lion engine and various minor modifications. Reconverted to a landplane, it flew in the 1924 King's Cup Air Race.

An unusual view of the Avro Type 552, displaying the early practice of marking the national 'G' upon the tailplane as well as the rudder. The Type 552 was one of a number of Avro designs produced in the immediate post-war years, aimed at the civilian market. Some of these aircraft, including the 552, were developments of the Avro 504 series.

Powered by an 80 h.p. Le Rhone, the Avro Type 554 was built for the Shackleton Antarctic Expedition of 1921. It was not used for this purpose, owing to the death of Shackleton, and eventually found its way to Newfoundland for seal spotting work.

The Avro 504 had many variants and was powered by several different engine types, while the basic airframe was in the main retained. This is a Canadian-built Avro 504O, with a Wright engine and single-float undercarriage, a design arrangement favoured by the American Navy.

The Fairey Fremantle was a four-seater long-range machine designed for a projected round-the-world flight, with a 650 h.p. Rolls-Royce Condor engine. It ended its career as a radio navigation development aircraft, in 1926.

The Fairey IIIC was the last of the Series III to be delivered before the Armistice, and the machine shown here, N2255, was the first of only five completed by the war's end. The engine was the 375 h.p. Rolls-Royce Eagle VIII and the type saw action in the Russian Expedition of 1919.

In the early 1920s, British aircraft manufacturers began to adapt wartime bomber aircraft as civil transports. The de Havilland Company converted the D.H.4 to the D.H.4A passenger aircraft in 1919, and in 1923 produced the D.H.50, which owed much to the D.H.9A bomber and featured a single pilot's seat and a passenger cabin under the centre section. The D.H.50 floatplane shown here was on trials for the Air Ministry, fitted with a Rolls-Royce engine and floats of improved and efficient design.

This close-up shows yet another version of the famous Avro 504; the 'O' model with twin floats, a radial engine, and cut-away centre-section incorporating external gravity fuel tanks. As previously illustrated, in Canada the 'O' was flown on a single central float.

The Avro Bison of 1921 was well-named, and the Napier Lion engine was hard put to haul this unwieldy structure through the air. The deep fuselage was built to house naval observers and wireless operators in unaccustomed comfort. These two views illustrate N9594, an early Bison I modified as an experimental floatplane with a single central float.

A contemporary of the Avro Bison was the Blackburn "Blackburn", both types being designed for naval spotting and reconnaissance duties and powered by the Napier Lion engine. Two Blackburns, N9828 illustrated, and N9833, were fitted with twin floats which had strengthened keels to enable landing on a carrier deck. Both these aircraft were early models, with the top wing attached directly to the fuselage.

The Blackburn Swift was built in 1919 as a single-seat torpedo aircraft intended for operation from carriers, its layout following that of the Sopwith Cuckoo and the Blackburn Blackbird. The engine was a 450 h.p. Napier Lion. Exhibited at Olympia in 1920, the Swift prototype, N139, attracted overseas orders, but none were built for the Fleet Air Arm. The machine may be regarded as the prototype for the Blackburn Dart, which it closely resembled.

The Lion-engined **Blackburn Dart** appeared in 1920, entering service with the Fleet Air Arm in 1923 and serving for ten years. On 1 July 1926, a Dart flown by Flt. Lt. Boyce made the first night landing on an aircraft carrier, touching down on H.M.S. *Furious*. Normally fitted with a land undercarriage, a number of Darts were modified with a second cockpit incorporating dual control and a twin-float undercarriage, and the civil-registered prototype, **G-EBKF**, is shown here.

The Fairey IIID was one of the leading types to the F.A.A. from 1924 to 1930. The aircraft seen here after a catapult launch, probably from H.M.S. *Vindictive,* is of an early batch powered by Rolls-Royce Eagle engines of 375 h.p.

This photograph was taken during the Royal Navy's Spring Cruise of 1930, off Gibraltar, and shows a late-series Fairey IIID with a Napier Lion engine being launched by catapult. The destroyer, just visible beyond the aircraft, was stationed aft of the launching ship in case of accidents. The crowd of spectators was not a usual gathering, but on this occasion the pilot was doing his first catapult "solo"! The IIID featured in the very first catapult launch of a standard F.A.A. floatplane on 30 October 1925, piloted by Wg. Cdr. Burling.

Fairey IIIF S1817 in position on the main armament turret of H.M.S. *Barham*, which was turned into wind for launching from the catapult. The IIIF was a classic and popular machine, employed widely by both the R.A.F. and the Fleet Air Arm.

The Fairey Flycatcher of 1923 was an immensely popular aircraft, strong and ideal for carrier operation and superb for aerobatics. The engine was a 400 h.p. Armstrong Siddeley Jaguar, which provided a loud and unique sound at full throttle. The machine shown here in flight over Grand Harbour, Valetta, Malta, is actually an amphibian, with the wheels protruding below the floats.

A Fairey Flycatcher taxies away from a ship after casting-off the crane sling used to lower it into the water. This particular aircraft may have been a floatplane or amphibian-floatplane, for both types were identical when viewed from above. By September 1930, the Fleet Air Arm had eight Flights of Flycatchers serving in *Courageous, Eagle, Hermes,* and *Glorious.*

Flycatcher S1297 leaving the
catapult of H.M.S.
Vindictive during trials that
took place in 1925. The
machine is fitted with floats
of improved shape and
constructed of metal. The
Flycatcher was finally made
obsolete in April 1935.

Experimental Blackburn Dart N204 was fitted with floats and modified to incorporate a gunner's position aft of the pilot. Normally a single-seater, several Darts were built with two cockpits for training purposes as floatplanes with the R.A.F. Reserve Training Schools.

The production version of the Blackburn Ripon was known as the Mk. IIA and entered service with the Fleet Air Arm in August 1929. A torpedo-bomber, the Ripon had twice the range of the earlier Dart and therefore carried an observer for navigational purposes. Two Ripons were fitted with floats, S1268 and S1468, the latter being illustrated here. The engine fitted was a 570 h.p. Napier Lion XIA.

The Parnall Peto was designed as a two-seater reconnaissance floatplane to operate by catapult from the Royal Navy submarine *M.2*, in which a special hangar was provided. N181, seen here, had a 135 h.p. Armstrong Siddeley Mongoose engine, as did the six production aircraft.

An Avro Wright floatplane of the Royal Canadian Air Force, photographed at Rockcliffe, Ontario, on 30 September 1925. This variant, fitted with a Wright engine and a single main float, was basically the Avro 504N, and the British twin-float equivalent became the "O" model of the 504. The machine illustrated had the civil registration G-CYGK.

48

The D.H.60 was the first of the famous de Havilland Moth series, and in R.A.F. service was powered by the Cirrus engine. The aircraft shown here had an experimental single-float undercarriage and a Gipsy engine. A D.H.60 of the R.A.F. was fitted with twin floats in 1935, and successfully located the missing explorer, Ellsworth, in the Antarctic.

The Short Sturgeon of 1927 was an experimental floatplane of all-metal construction intended for the R.A.F., and powered by a 450 h.p. Bristol Jupiter radial engine. It had a somewhat unusual arrangement for the crew, with its three cockpits. The sole prototype, N199, was extensively tested, but was not accepted for production.

The Blackburn Bluebird of 1930 was a light sporting or trainer aircraft which featured side-by-side seating for the two occupants, and this arrangement was retained in the successful Blackburn B.2 Trainer and Tourer aircraft of 1932. At least one Bluebird was tested as a floatplane, and G-EBSW is shown here on its ground-handling trolley.

In 1931, Short Brothers of Rochester produced the Gurnard amphibian as a version of the 1929 floatplane of the same name, fitting it experimentally with an amphibian undercarriage developed for use on light aircraft. The wheels were arranged to swing forwards and upwards in the retracted position. The engine was a Rolls-Royce Kestrel of 525 h.p.

The first production models of the D.H.87 Hornet Moth appeared in August 1935. and during the next three years 165 were built, powered by the 130 h.p. Gipsy engine. The Hornet Moth quickly became popular throughout the world, for nearly half of the production machines were exported. D.H. Aircraft of Canada fitted the machine with Fairchild floats and an up-rated 145 h.p. Gipsy Major engine, and four such aircraft were submitted to the British Air Ministry for evaluation as floatplane trainers.

Fairey IIIF floatplanes of No. 47 (Bomber) Squadron in formation during a visit to Malta in the early 1930s. Developed progressively from the Fairey IIIA of 1917, the IIIF was built in some numbers, second only to the Hawker Hart variants.

The Fairey IIIF prototype displays its clean and sturdy lines. Serialled N198, the machine made its maiden flight as a landplane from Northolt on 19 March 1926, piloted by Capt. Norman Macmillan. After further test flights, Macmillan delivered the aircraft to Hamble, where it was converted to a floatplane, as shown here, and flown from the Hamble river on 20 April 1926.

Fairey IIIF Mk. II S1251 is lowered into the water by crane, with its engine running. The IIIF Mks. I to III were all three-seaters destined for the Fleet Air Arm, whereas the Mk. IV was a two-seat bomber for the R.A.F., both services operating the machine as a land or marine type. The Mk. II engine was a Napier Lion XI.

Designed as a single-seater fighter and fitted with a 215 h.p. Armstrong Siddeley Lynx engine, the Avro Type 584 Avocet was the first all-metal stress-skinned aircraft produced by this company. It was built in 1926, and featured easily-removed wings for stowage purposes. No production was undertaken, but Avro gained a great deal of useful experience in this type of construction.

The Short S.22 Scion Senior, with four 90 h.p. Pobjoy Niagara engines, was actually a half-scale model of the S.23 Empire Flying-Boat, and provided much useful aerodynamic information. Four of these aircraft were built in 1935-36.

The Fairey Gordon was a conversion of the R.A.F. IIIF MI. IVB, the Lion engine being replaced by a 525 h.p. Armstrong Siddeley Panther radial. The F.A.A. equivalent of the Gordon was known as the Seal, illustrated here on its ground trolley.

The Fairey IIIF Mk. III saw a change from the previous mixed wood and metal construction to one of all-metal, and the IIIF Mk. IIIM was followed by the IIIF Mk. IIIB. An example of this variant, S1502, is seen here in flight. The Mk. IIIB, retaining the Lion engine, had a strengthened fuselage for catapulting and a number of detail changes. The IIIF had a long service life, and was not declared obsolete until 1940.

A Fairey Seal being launched from the slipway at Calshot. Seals were flown in both the marine and land-plane configurations, entering service with the Fleet Air Arm in 1933, and remaining with some Squadrons until the outbreak of World War II, while in other units it was replaced by the Blackburn Shark. The float-plane version was employed by warship catapult Flights.

The Hawker Dantorp was a development of the Horsley torpedo-bomber, ordered by the Danish Government in 1930. Two aircraft were built, Nos. 201 and 202, and, initially flown with the 800 h.p. Armstrong Siddeley Leopard II engine, were delivered in 1933 with the 805 h.p. Leopard IIIA. The Dantorp was operated by a crew of three, having interchangeable wheels and floats, and is seen here at Felixstowe in 1932.

A second view of the Hawker Dantorp at Felixstowe. In Danish service the two machines were allocated to the the 1st *Luftofltille* as the HB.III, following service on Fleet co-operation with the 9th Airgroup, and with the outbreak of World War II saw much flying on mine-spotting and neutrality patrols. In 1940, after the German occupation of Denmark, the 1st *Luftflotille* was deactivated and the aircraft stored at Copenhagen, where they were destroyed by sabotage in November 1943.

Alan Cobham made many long-distance flights, but his greatest took place in 1926, when he flew from London to Australia and back. His aircraft was a D.H.50, G-EBFO, fitted with a 385 h.p. Armstrong Siddeley Jaguar engine and a float undercarriage, the latter being exchanged for wheels during the trans-Australia leg of the journey. Cobham left England on 30 June, and is seen here alighting on the Thames after the 28,000-mile flight on 1 October. A few days later, Alan Cobham was knighted for this and other achievements.

The Short S.11 Valetta was the largest floatplane of its day, and was built in 1929-30 to an Air Ministry order for comparison with the flying-boat. Powered by three 525 h.p. Bristol Jupiters and registered G-AAJY, the Valetta was flown by Sir Alan Cobham on a 12,300-mile African survey flight in 1931.

The Short Valetta moored on the Medway, Rochester. Only one machine was built, in an unique and unusual configuration for a British aircraft, and it was also flown at Croydon with a wheeled undercarriage for further evaluation.

In the 1923 Schneider Trophy contest, the British Supermarine Sea Lion III flying-boat was beaten by the two American Curtiss C.R.3 floatplanes, and the Supermarine designer, Reginald Mitchell, turned his attention to the design of a streamlined racing floatplane for the 1925 contest. The engine chosen was a special short-life 700 h.p. Napier Lion. This beautifully clean monoplane was the result, and the Supermarine S.4 began a whole line of British Schneider Trophy racers.

Side view of the Supermarine S.4. Apart from some metal fittings, the aircraft was constructed entirely of wood, with a plywood covering over a monocoque fuselage and cantilever wings, the latter incorporating Lamblin radiators on the undersurface.

The 1925 Schneider Trophy contest was held at Baltimore, U.S.A., and the S.4 is seen here taxi-ing out for the mandatory trials, with Capt. Henri Biard at the controls. Shortly after, the S.4 crashed due to wing flutter.

The Supermarine S.5 embodied all the lessons learnt from the S.4, and was built for the 1927 contest at Venice. Three S.5s were constructed, N219, N220, and N221, with metal fuselages and floats, the wings being of wood. N219 had a direct-drive Lion engine, while those of N220 and N221 were geared. In the race, Fg. Off. S. N. Webster took the Trophy in N220 at an average speed of 281.65 m.p.h., while Flt. Lt. Worseley came second in N219 at 273.01 m.p.h.

The S.4 on the works slipway at Woolston, Southampton. Before its departure for America, the machine captured the World air speed record for marine aircraft, and also the British record, at a speed of 226.75 m.p.h.

The Short Crusader, N226, was reserve aircraft for the 1927 contest. It was powered by a 960 h.p. Bristol Mercury engine in a helmeted cowling, and went to Venice in H.M.S. *Eagle.* The machine crashed due to crossed aileron control cables.

N250 was one of two Gloster VI Golden Arrow machines built for the 1927 Schneider Trophy, but both were withdrawn due to trouble with their 1,320 h.p. Napier Lion engines. However, one machine established a world record of 336 m.p.h.

Supermarine S.5 N219 taking-off for its first test flight at Calshot in 1927. On this first S.5, the enormous engine torque was balanced by making one float longer than the other, but this was found unnecessary for the other two S.5s.

A fine view of the Gloster VI Golden Arrow, showing the elliptical plan-form of the wings and the careful streamlining of the three Napier Lion cylinder banks. The machine derived its name from its colour of overall gold. The two Gloster VIs were used as trainers by the R.A.F. High Speed Flight for the 1931 Schneider contest, and were serialled N249 and N250. Their maximum speed was 351 m.p.h.

The Gloster IV was built for the 1927 Schneider contest at Venice, and had a 900 h.p. Napier Lion engine. The IV, N224, was followed by the IVA, N222, and IVB, N223. The IVB flew in the contest, but after attaining 277 m.p.h. retired on the 5th lap.

Two Supermarine S.6 aircraft were built for the 1929 race, and serialled N247 and N248, the latter being shown here. The S.6s were the first machines to be powered by the new Rolls-Royce 'R' engine of 1,900 h.p., and ancestor of the famous Merlin. In 1931, this engine was modified to provide no less than 2,300 h.p. Flown by Fg. Off. Waghorn, N247 took the Trophy for Britain on 7 September 1929 at a speed of 328 m.p.h.

A fine view of Supermarine S.5 N219. After use as a trainer in 1929, this aircraft was returned to the works and fitted with a new geared Napier Lion engine, having been selected as reserve aircraft for the 1929 contest at Spithead. Flown by Flt. Lt. D'Arcy Greig, N219 took third place in the race at a speed of 282.11 m.p.h.

Flt. Lt. Waghorn under tow in Supermarine S.6 N247. As well as winning the 1929 contest, this aircraft, fitted with a propeller of altered pitch, set up a World speed record of 355.8 m.p.h. on 10 September 1929 and 357.7 m.p.h. two days later, in the hands of Sqn. Ldr. Orlebar. In similar fashion to its stable-mate, N248, N247 was modified to S.6A standard, but suffered from tail flutter.

The Gloster VI, N249, which established a world
speed record of 336 m.p.h. on 10 September 1929.
On one run, it reached a maximum speed of 351.6
m.p.h. The engine was a 1,320 h.p. Lion VIID.

Supermarine S.6, N248, with its handling party.
This machine was the first to receive the uprated
Rolls-Royce 'R' engine of 2,300 h.p., and together
with longer floats became the S.6A.

The Gloster IVA, N222. The IVA and IVB were
smaller overall than the original IV, and had a
ventral fin fitted under the rear fuselage. These
machines had a colouring of blue and bronze.

N
220

N
247

The 1931 Schneider Trophy contest was crucial for Britain in that a third successive win would mean retention of the Trophy for all time. Economic depression caused the Government to withdraw its support, but Lady Houston generously donated sufficient funds for the construction of two Supermarine S.6Bs, S1595 and S1596, the latter being shown here. Powered by the 2,300 h.p. Rolls-Royce 'R' engine, S1595 won the Trophy outright at 340.08 m.p.h. piloted by **Flt. Lt. Boothman**, and S1596 set up a new World's record of 407.5 m.p.h., flown by **Flt. Lt. Stainforth.**

◁

Comparative side-views of two Schneider Trophy winners: above, Supermarine S.5 N220, tenth contest at Venice, 1927, and below, Supermarine S.6 N247, eleventh contest at Spithead, 1929. Most noticeable is the difference in engine cowlings and thrust lines between the Napier Lion of N220 and the Rolls-Royce 'R' of N247, also the propeller sizes and pitch.

The Short S.11 Valetta in flight over the Medway at Rochester. This most unusual British aircraft was flown by Sir Alan Cobham on an African survey flight between July and September 1931, alighting on Lakes Albert, Victoria, Kivu and Edward. The Valetta was shown at the 1932 Hendon Air Pageant and subsequently employed by the Air Ministry for testing radio equipment.

The de Havilland Company, already with an overseas subsidiary in Australia, formed a Canadian branch in 1928 as de Havilland Aircraft of Canada, Ltd., at Mount Dennis, Ontario. The new company imported a number of D.H. machines from Britain, adapting, and later building them to Canadian requirements. The D.H. 84 Dragon shown here arrived in 1933, followed by the D.H.89 Dragon Rapide.

Last of the Blackburn torpedo-carrying biplanes for the **F.A.A.**, the Shark appeared in 1934, fitted with a 700 h.p. Armstrong Siddeley Tiger engine and featuring a Warren Girder wing-strut arrangement. The prototype illustrated, K4295, was originally the private venture Blackburn B-6, and the machine was designed for an interchangeable wheel or float undercarriage. A total of 238 Sharks were built.

An impressive view of two Blackburn Sharks at the Brough works in March 1936. Together with four others, these aircraft were built for the Portuguese Navy, and were photographed just prior to their acceptance trials. The Shark could carry bombs or a torpedo, and the wings were arranged to fold for shipboard use. The type was also in service as a floatplane with the Royal Canadian Air Force.

One of the Blackburn Sharks ordered by the Portuguese Navy taxi-ing at speed. Not a very pretty aircraft, the Shark had great strength, and the wings could be folded with a full bomb-load of 1,500 pounds in the wing racks.

The Short S.20 "Mercury" was the upper component of the Mayo composite aircraft, with four Napier-Halford Rapier V engines. On 8 October 1938, "Mercury" was air-launched for a non-stop flight of 6,045 miles, an existing World record.

The two Mayo Composite components on the Medway at Rochester. The lower portion comprised a modified Short Empire Boat, powered by four 915 h.p. Bristol Pegasus XC engines and named "Maia". The first combined flight was made on 4 January 1938, and the first airborne separation on 6 February. The principle behind the scheme was that "Mercury" could be air-launched by "Maia" while loaded to a weight in excess of its individual take-off capability, thus achieving absolute maximum range.

CF-BFF

Last in the line of successful twin-engined biplanes designed by the de Havilland company was the scaled-down D.H. 90 Dragonfly, aimed at the wealthy private owner or business executive. The sixth production aircraft was shipped to Canada and flown in Ontario during June 1936. The aircraft illustrated above and opposite was the only Dragonfly to be fitted with floats, and so equipped, made its maiden flight at Longueuil, Quebec, on 21 July 1937, and was finally written off in 1949. The engines were 130 h.p. Gipsy Majors.

Most famous of all British naval aircraft, the Fairey Swordfish began its life in 1934 as the T.S.R.II, powered by a 690 h.p. Bristol Pegasus engine. Known affectionally as the "Stringbag", the type was flown as either a land or floatplane.

The Swordfish prototype, K4190, taking-off as a floatplane at Hamble in November 1934. K4190 later underwent catapult trails aboard H.M.S. *Repulse*. By early 1940 the parent company had delivered 692 Swordfish, out of a total of

First flown in 1936, the
Fairey Seafox was designed
as a reconnaissance
floatplane for catapulting
from cruisers, and was
fitted with a 395 h.p. Napier
Rapier engine. Altogether
64 Seafox aircraft were
delivered, serving in the
early days of World War II.

The Seafox had a short
operational life, but it
found a niche in aviation
history by the action of one
aircraft which flew from
H.M.S. *Ajax* during the
Battle of the River Plate on
13 December 1939. The pilot
was Lt. Lewin, who received
the D.S.C.

Hawker Osprey K3629 leaving the catapult of H.M.S. *Sussex.* With a Rolls-Royce Kestrel IIMS engine of 525 h.p., the Osprey had a maximum speed of 169 m.p.h. as a floatplane, which was considerably better than the performance of the Fairey IIIF which it replaced in all catapult Flights. The machine was armed with a fixed Vickers gun and a moveable Lewis in the rear cockpit, being classed as a fighter reconnaissance aircraft.

S1700 was the second Osprey III, featuring stainless steel primary structure and a 630 h.p. Kestrel engine. This aircraft was experimentally modified with a single central float of Armstrong-Whitworth construction, and was also flown with a Short Brothers float. S1700 underwent prolonged handling and performance trials until 1937, when it was damaged in a beaching accident, following which it went to R.A.F. Cranwell as an instructional airframe.

The Queen Bee was a special radio-controlled version of the D.H. Tiger Moth for anti-aircraft gunnery practice by the Royal Navy, entering service with the Navy, and the R.A.F., in 1935. This photograph was taken on 15 June 1939 from H.M.S. *Shropshire*, off Alexandria, and shows Queen Bee K8652 being launched by catapult for what was to be her last flight, as she was shot down on this run. 420 Queen Bee aircraft were built.

D. H. Dragon Rapide CF-AEO, photographed at Rockcliffe, Ontario on 3 July 1935. This aircraft type proved to be the most successful and economic aircraft ever to be used in Canada, being operated on wheels, floats and skis. The Rapide was in extensive use by Canadian Pacific Airlines, Quebec Airways Ltd., and Maritime Central Airways, as well as by many small charter companies operating in the bush-flying sphere.

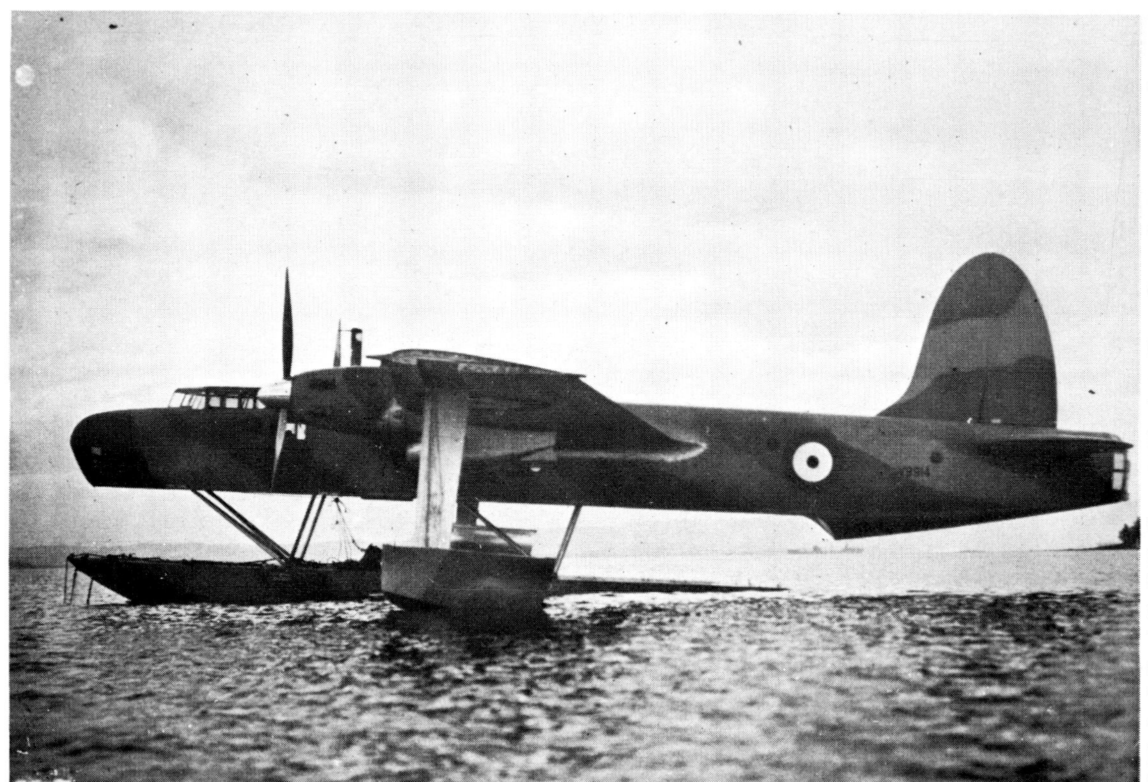

The Blackburn B.20 of 1940 was an attempt to link the floatplane and the flying-boat for the purpose of maximum efficiency, and to this end the planing bottom of the hull was arranged as a retractable pontoon, in combination with retractable wing-tip floats. With three gun positions and a 2,000-pound bomb load proposed, the B.20 had an estimated performance of over 300 m.p.h. The machine, serialled V8914, was fitted with twin Rolls-Royce Vulture engines of 1,720 h.p., and was lost with all on board in a crash on a trial flight from Dumbarton.

Following success with the Spitfire Mk. VB floatplane conversions, and a limited production in 1942, the company involved, Folland Aircraft Ltd., of Hamble, were asked to make a further conversion, this time of Spitfire IX MJ982, and this aircraft is shown taking-off. Although much flying was done, none of the Spitfire floatplanes saw active service.

The Supermarine Spitfire owed much in the design field to the Schneider Trophy racing floatplanes, and in 1940 an historical reversion was made by trials of float-equipped Spitfires for use in the Norwegian campaign. This photograph is of Mk. VB, W3760, the first Spitfire floatplane to be flown. Later, the fin shape was modified.

The Bristol Bolingbroke was constructed by firms in Canada, and served with the R.C.A.F. as a bomber-reconnaissance aircraft. It was, in fact, identical to the Blenheim IV. One machine was tested on floats, but not used on operations.

The prototype Airspeed Queen Wasp, K8888, in flight. Designed to replace the Queen Bee pilotless target aircraft, the machine had a 350 h.p. Armstrong Siddeley Cheetah engine. In the event, in 1940 targets were plentiful and production cancelled.

In 1963, the Seaplane Club
was founded in this country,
with Sir Francis Chichester
as Vice President and
founder member. The Club
flew this Tiger Moth as the
"Sea Tiger" from the R.N.
Station at Lee-on-Solent,
in Hampshire.

Another view of CF-AEO,
the Canadian D.H.89 Dragon
Rapide illustrated earlier.
The extension to the tail fin
may be noted; this was a
modification by the de
Havilland Canadian company
to allow aerodynamically
for the fitment of floats, as
on the Dragonfly.

The Auster light monoplanes were well-known during World War II for their work as artillery spotters and as light communications aircraft. The post-war model was the Auster A.O.P. (Air Observation Post) 6, with a Gipsy Major engine. Two of these machines accompanied the R.A.F. Antarctic Expedition of 1949-50 fitted out as floatplanes, and one is seen here flying near the Expedition ship.

Two views of the prototype Auster A.O.P.6 on floats in March 1947. The engine was a 145 h.p. Gipsy Major VII, which replaced the American Lycoming fitted to earlier models. There were several other improvements, including the introduction of auxiliary aerofoil flaps below and aft of the trailing edges of the wings. The Auster 6 served the A.O.P. Squadrons in Korea and Malaya.

Thankfully preserved for posterity, Supermarine S.6B S1596 is shown here on exhibition at Abingdon. This historic machine is housed in the Science Museum, South Kensington, together with an example of its illustrious descendant —a Battle of Britain Spitfire.